Joy In Every Footstep

A Journey of Spiritual Poetry

Ron Tranmer Poetry

For information about bulk purchase discounts or licensing poems for commercial use, visit www.rontranmer.com.

ISBN: 978-0-9894439-6-8

Printed in the United States of America

All poems by Ron Tranmer
Design: Ryan Tranmer, Rise Design
Images licensed through Fotolia.com & iStock

"Poetry"

There's a bit of magic in the rhythm and rhyme of poetry. It can touch hearts in a way that awakens and enhances our inner feelings.

Although some of my verses of poetry may not coincide perfectly with your religious beliefs, it is my hope that many will touch your heart and open your mind to the love of God, our Father In Heaven, and His Son, Jesus Christ.

– Ron Tranmer

A Bit About Me

I was born in Jerome Idaho in 1940. In 1961, shortly after returning from a three-year tour in the Marines, I fell in love with, and married, Carolynn "Joy" Deuel, a four feet eleven inch angel, who, after fifty three years of marriage, is still the love of my life. We have three daughters and a son who have blessed our lives with thirteen grandchildren. They, in turn, have blessed us with ten great-grandchildren.

Over the years I have written more than 400 poems. Many are licensed and can be found on wall plaques, woven throws, cups, wind chimes, bookmarks, music boxes and even headstones.

In our walk through life, we will find happiness and joy; climb hills and face storms; But it is through our faith in Heavenly Father and His Son, Jesus Christ, and the knowledge of Their great and everlasting love, that we find "Joy In Every Footstep".

Look for my new book of remembrance poetry:
"One by One The Chain Will Link Again"...

One by One
The Chain Will Link Again
Poems of Comfort, Hope, & Remembrance

Ron Tranmer
AUTHOR OF "BROKEN CHAIN"

Rocking Chairs
in Heaven
Poetry of Comfort, Hope & Remembrance
for those grieving the loss of a child

Ron Tranmer
AUTHOR OF "HAPPY BIRTHDAY IN HEAVEN"

...and my book of child loss poetry:
"Rocking Chairs In Heaven"

Index

Index

A Gift Of Love

God gave us beautiful flowers
and tall majestic trees.
The warming rays of sunshine
and the coolness of a breeze.

Bright rainbows of all colors
that please the human eye.
And endless twinkling stars
that shine brightly in the sky .

The seashore and the oceans
ever rolling waves of blue.
Then from above, a gift of love...
He blessed the world with You!

A Grain Of Sand

I'm as a single grain of sand
upon a vast seashore.

I'm as a drop of water
In the ocean... Nothing more.

I'm but one in seven billion
In this world whereon I trod.

But I am known and loved
by my Savior... and my God.

A Love Beyond Compare

I often look up to the sky
and ask my Lord and Savior why
He would suffer, bleed and die
for someone such as I.

For my sins did Christ atone.
His sacrifice for me has shown
the greatest love I've ever known.
A love beyond compare.

Although nothing could repay
the gift he gave upon that day,
I will live in such a way
He'll see my gratitude.

Then when I die my soul will flee
and I shall live eternally
because of what He did for me.
All Glory To His name.

A Prayer For My Son

Dear Lord, Your gifts are many
and I'm grateful for each one.
I especially want to thank You
for the gift of my dear son.

No parent could be prouder.
No son could bring more joy.
And no one in this big wide world
is loved more than my boy.

I thank You for his precious life.
Watch over him I pray.
Keep him safe, and free from harm
with every passing day.

Give him strength and wisdom.
Life's battles may he win.
And may he know how much he's loved,
I humbly pray ... Amen

Angelic Mothers

Loving gifts from Heavenly Father,
to His children here on earth.
Sweet Angels sent from Heaven
who come down to give us birth.

You teach us, and you guide us
with encouragement and praise.
And love us unconditionally
throughout your earthly days.

In my heart I know
there will never be another,
more treasured, loved and cherished
than you... My Beautiful Mother.

As He Would Do

Our future is determined
by the choices that we make.
Wise ones lead to happiness.
Poor ones bring heartache.

Satan's lures may tempt us
and he'll have us if we bite;
But we will follow Christ ,The Lord,
whose way is truth and light.

Through darkness and temptation
His love will guide us through,
when we choose to walk with Him
and do "As He Would Do."

Best Friend

Although my friends are many,
I'll tell you something true.
I've never ever had a friend
as wonderful as you.

You are, without a doubt,
the greatest friend I've ever had.
Always there, no matter where,
through the good and bad.

Even when I've hurt you
by the things I do or say,
You are always so forgiving
and never walk away.

I know that I can count on you
forever, without end.
You are my Heavenly Father,
My Lord ...and my best friend.

Bless My Soldier

Dear God, who dwells in heaven,
hear my humble fervent prayer.
Watch over my dear soldier boy
and keep him in your care.

I'm trying not to worry,
and he writes that all is well,
but if ever he's in danger,
he most likely wouldn't tell.

He was raised to know You.
Do You hear from him each day?
Lord, please guide his footsteps
and keep him from harms way.

May he feel our love surround him.
Strong and brave may he be.
Then, when he's served his country,
bring him safely home to me.

Brother & Friend

To me it makes no difference
the color of your skin.
Outside doesn't matter.
What's important is within.

We are all God's children.
None favored over others;
And since He is our father,
we are sisters and we're brothers.

Should in life we chance to meet,
my hand I will extend;
And from that very moment
I will have another friend.

Cloud Of Love

True experience, Written by my wife, Carolynn

While resting on my patio
and gazing at the sky;
I said, "I love You Lord",
as a cloud went drifting by.

Then at that very moment
and giving me a start ,
that little cloud changed its shape
and formed a perfect heart.

My eyes began to fill with tears
for then and there I knew,
God shaped that cloud into a heart
to say, "I love you too".

Counting Blessings

How I longed for sleep
as I lie there in my bed;
But the weight of all my worries
kept me wide-awake instead.

I tossed and then I turned,
but sleep was not to be.
And when I started counting sheep
they ran away from me.

But then a sudden feeling
in my heart began to swell.
It was as an angel whispered,
"Be at peace. All is well."

I forgot about the troubles
that were swimming in my head,
and began to think of all the
blessings in my life instead.

Contentment filled my soul
and I soon fell fast asleep,
because worry saw my blessings
and ran off with the sheep.

David And Goliath

The bible tells the story
of a giant with a sword,
who believed that he was greater
than man, or God, our Lord.

Feared by those he challenged,
though their God this man defied;
This giant, named Goliath,
had Saul's army terrified.

Then came a Shepard boy,
who without a shred of fear,
said he would fight the giant,
and with God he'd persevere.

Without armor, shield, or sword,
but with faith unwavering;
Young David faced Goliath
with a pebble and a sling.

The pebble found its mark
and struck Goliath at his head.
And because of faith in God,
the giant fell before them...Dead!

Deeds Of Love

With Ears, hear My word.
With Feet, follow Me.
With Hands, do My work,

Today and endlessly.

With Mouth, teach My gospel.
With Head, bow in prayer.
With Heart, show compassion

To My children everywhere.

With Eyes be ever searching
looking for another's needs.
Let the love you have for Me
be shown through loving deeds.

Dishes And Floors

The dishes are stacked
high in the sink.
The dishwasher's loaded
clear up to the brink.

Her vacuum is idle.
Crumbs lie on the floor.
What's so important
these tasks she'd ignore?

Can she not see
her kitchen's a mess.
It almost seems as
she couldn't care less.

"Where to now child?
I'll try not to peek,.
I've counted to ten...
Now I'm coming to seek."

Somewhere in Heaven
high up above,
God's smiling to see
such motherly love.

More important to her
than dishes and floors,
is the treasure of time
with the child she adores.

Exhale

Breathing is important.
Of that, there is no doubt.
We must take the good air in,
and let the bad air out.

Yet there are some who don't exhale
the bad air as they should.
It stays inside and makes it hard
to inhale air that's good.

The air of pride and selfishness;
Contention, greed and sin,
will choke out all our good air
and corrupt us from within.

So, if the air you've taken in
is sinful, old, and stale;
Good, pure cleansing air awaits,
if only you'll exhale.

Families

Families, like ours,

Are strong and

Mighty in spirit.

In every moment of this

Life we will stand together

In righteousness. And with

Every opportunity, we will

Strive to serve our God.

Family Tree

There's love within our family tree
and happiness abounds.
Its roots are deeply planted
in rich and fertile grounds.

We enjoy the rays of sunshine
and endure the winds and rain.
And when a leaf falls from our tree,
together, we share the pain.

God gave us loving families
and never did intend,
that bonds of love built on earth,
upon our death should end.

For when, in time, we cross the veil,
how great our joy will be
as we greet loved ones waiting there
on Heaven's Family Tree.

*Fear is but a coward that
quickly runs and hides
from every living person
where faith in God resides.*

Fearless

*I have not feared life
and I have no fear of death.
I'll be at peace upon the day
I breathe my final breath.*

*For I have done my best
to live life righteously.
In life I walked with God.
In death He'll walk with me.*

Find The Time

Find the time to find the joy
found in serving one another.
Find the time to show compassion
to each sister and each brother.

Find the time to help another
who could use a helping hand;
And the time for understanding
those whom you don't understand.

Find time to bring some sunshine
to one who's sad and blue...
And God will find the time to pour
His blessings out to you.

Finger Pointing

When you point a finger,
If that's something that you do...
Remember three more on your hand
are pointing back at you.

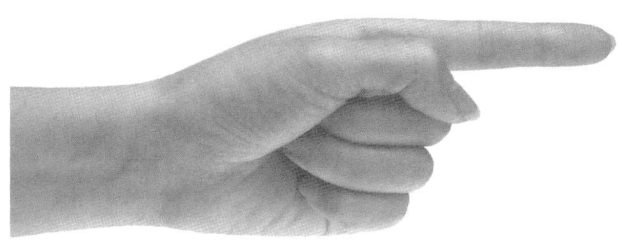

G.P.S.

Life is as a highway
and we are as a car.
Our journey may be short,
or one that's long and far.

There are many different roads
which take us here or there.
Some are very dangerous.
Let us choose each one with care.

*Watch for every **"Warning"** sign*
you see along the way.
*Take each road with **"Caution"***
and do not be led astray.

*Upon seeing, **"Do Not Enter"**,*
*think, **"Don't enter into sin"**.*
***"Yield"** not to temptation,*
*but, **"Keep Right"** and follow Him.*

*When we are at a **"Crossroad"**,*
*we must **"Stop"**, and there decide.*
***"Straight Ahead"**, or should we **"Turn"**?*
Sometimes we need a guide .

When our destination's Heaven,
life's roads are not a guess.
*We have **G**od's **P**recious **S**on.*
*Let Him be our **G.P.S**.*

God's Colors

Earth wouldn't be as beautiful
if all God's flowers were blue.
If rainbows were all yellow
that would be a sad thing too.

Suppose the ocean and the sky
were both the color white.
And everyone on Earth wore black.
Now, that would be a sight.

All of God's creations
are colored differently,
to give the world splendor
and to add variety.

To judge a person by their race
is sinful and a shame.
for we are all Gods children
and He loves us all the same.

God's Light

God made the stars
then touched each one
to brighten up the night.
The lost can find direction
and guidance from their light.

And should our spirits
lose their way, because
our path grows dim;
God's ever shining light awaits
to lead us back to Him.

Grateful Lips

Every day's a gift from God
and one to celebrate,
regardless of the challenges
we find upon our plate.

Everyone upon the earth
has challenges and trials.
Some endure complaining.
Others through their smiles.

Just think about our Savior
and the pain that He endured.
He suffered all for you and me
with no complaining word.

So as we travel down life's road,
amid its ruts and dips,
may thankfulness, and not complaint,
pass through our grateful lips.

Hand In Hand

Hand in Hand we'll walk together
throughout this earthly life,
and find joy in every footstep
that we take as man and wife.

We'll stop to smell the roses
as we journey side by side.
Our Love will be our strength
and Our God will be our guide.

We'll climb each hill along the way
and every one we'll conquer;
Knowing that life's challenges
will make our love grow stronger.

Then when our journey's ended,
God will open wide His door,
and we'll walk the streets of heaven
"Hand In Hand" forevermore.

Hand & Footprints

My Savior, Oh
how *bittersweet*,
the prints upon
Thy *hands* & *feet*.

Bitter, for the
pain Thou bore, that
we might live
forevermore.

Yet *sweet*,
as a reminder of...
The *greatness* of
Thy unmatched *love*.

Heaven's Door

When I knock on heaven's door
will angels let me in?
Will God see the good in me
and overlook my sin?

Will those I love, there above,
the ones who went before;
Welcome me with open arms
as I walk through the door?

Or with great tears, will they wave
and bid me there goodbye?
Lord help me... to worthy be,
when it's my time to die.

Heaven's Light

The sun shines down upon us
with rays of warmth and light.
Then when the day has ended,
disappears beyond our sight.

We then are left in darkness,
not because the sun has died,
but because it's shining brightly
on the world's other side.

So it is when those we love
come to their end of days.
They go on to the other side
to shine their loving rays.

That's why Heaven is a place
that glows beyond compare.
The lights of those who've left us
are all brightly shining there.

Heaven's Suitcase

A Sunday teacher asked a boy,
A lad of only seven,
"What would you take with you
if God called you up to Heaven?"

He thought for but a moment,
and this was his reply;
"I'd take mommy and my daddy."
The teacher asked him why.

"Well, Mommy's always busy
doing things she needs to do.
And daddy can't play catch
because he's always busy too.

If we were up in Heaven
how happy I would be,
'cause if they weren't so busy
they could spend some time with me."

****

The parents of this little child would live their lives in sorrow
if God, who gave this lad to them took him away tomorrow.

There is little more important, in the eyes of God above,
than time spent with our children building lasting bonds of love.

****

He Stands At The Door

He stands at the door and knocks.
Shall we open and let Him come in?
Are we hiding behind its locks,
Unwilling because of our sin?

He knocks at the door to our heart.
He can heal, and make us whole.
Opening our door is the start.
He'll bring joy and peace to our soul.

His love for us keeps Him out there.
He patiently waits where He stands.
If we wonder, "Does He really care?";
We can look at the prints in His hands.

He suffered and died on a cross.
Our sins He willingly bore.
His love is real, and ready to heal
if we'll only open our door.

Hide & Seek

We are all God's children.
Some strong, and others weak.
He knows who really loves Him
by life's game of Hide and Seek.

Some "Seek" His words and will,
and want to do what's right,
While others "Hide" and shun Him,
though He shines His guiding light.

He hopes that all will seek Him
and not be the hiding kind,
for in Him there's great treasure;
Which all who seek shall find.

His Sheep

When we follow our dear Savior
we're as sheep of His fold.
He knows us and will lead us,
as in scripture we are told.

The Savior, as our Shepard,
will surround us with His love.
He'll guide us and watch over us
and bless us from above.

May we never, ever, wonder
from His flock and become prey
to that wolf, whose name is Satan,
who would lead us all astray.

But be safe and never perish,
for when righteously we stand,
Satan, that old devil,
cannot pluck us from His hand.

As we follow our dear Shepard
what blessings we shall reap,
in the pastures of His kingdom
as His faithful, loyal sheep.

(John 10: 27, 28)
*"My sheep hear my voice, and I know them, and
they follow me: And I give unto them eternal life;
and they shall never perish, neither shall any man
pluck them out of my hand."*

Holy Scriptures

As you read
the **holy scriptures**
may your soul
be gratified.
And may you feel
God's presence
in your heart
and by your side.

From Holy,
sacred verses
may you
grow and may
you learn.
And may you
feel of His
great love
with **every**
page you
turn.

How Are You?

When someone smiles and greets you
with a friendly, "How are you"?
Think about that question
from another point of view.

How are you... using time
God gives you every day?

How are you... making certain
you're not wasting it away?

How are you... showing others
in your heart you really care?

When they need a helping hand,
How are you... at being there?

How are you... overcoming
life's temptations laced with sin?

How are you... telling Satan
that he's not invited in?

Each time you hear that greeting
may your conscience proudly shine;

So when you're ask, **"How are you"**,
you can say... "I'm doing fine".

How Great

How great Thy love, my Savior.
How great Thy sacrifice.
That I might have eternal life,
Thou paid an awful price.

How great Thy pain and suffering,
on a cross at Calvary.
May I live life worthy, Lord,
of what Thou did for me.

I Imagine Heaven

I imagine Heaven
as a peaceful, happy place;
Where joy and contentment
puts a smile on every face.

I imagine many mansions
and streets of shining gold.
Never being sick again,
and never growing old.

I imagine Heaven
as a paradise above.
A perfect place where every heart
is filled with pure, sweet love.

I believe that heaven
is a place where hopes come true.
A place where I'll forever share
eternity with you.

If Ye Love Me

We've received a gift so great
we never could repay.
But if we ask our Savior how,
I'm certain He would say:

"I suffered, bled, and died for you
because I love you so.
Let your actions show your gratitude;
Then in my heart I'll know. "

(John 14: 15)
"If ye love me, keep My commandments"

Life Complete

*Live each and every single day
as though it were your last.
Look only to the future
and forget about the past.*

*Be caring, kind, and thoughtful
to everyone you meet.
Live by Christ's example
and your life will be complete.*

Life's Garden

*Life is as a garden
and requires tender care.
The seeds we choose determine
how great the splendor there.*

*We must nurture, feed and water;
and watch over it each day.
Noxious weeds must be cut down
so they won't grow and stay.*

*And every gardener who is wise
knows rule number one...*
"A garden is more beautiful
when nourished by *The Son*."

Look Inside

If we could look inside the hearts
of everyone we know,
we'd see the inner person
and our love for them would grow.

We'd know each trial they have faced.
Each burden they have bore.
Yes, with just one look inside
we'd love them so much more.

It is easy to judge others
from impressions they impart,
but we can't really know them
'til we know what's in their heart.

Let's remember, we're God's children.
We are sister, and we're brother.
Let us look inside each other's heart
with love for one another.

Look Up

Look up
*When life is getting you down
and you are sad and blue.*

Look up
*And know that God above
is watching over you.*

Look up
*When heartaches come your way
and seem to fill your cup.*

*His sweet love will bring you peace
if only you'll*
Look Up

Love's Greatest Test

He doesn't know her anymore
but she knows who he is.
Her husband, and her sweetheart,
and the father of their kids.

She made a humble vow to him
upon their wedding day,
that she would love and cherish,
and honor come what may.

There is no greater test of love,
or greater lesson learned;
than that from they who give such love
though it is not returned.

Alzheimer's robbed his memory
and took him far away,
but all will be restored in full
on resurrection day.

Then what heartfelt gratitude
that day will be expressed
by he, who's faithful sweetheart,
passed love's greatest test.

Mother Nature

Have you looked out at the ocean
as waves crash to the shore,
and felt the awesome power
of it's great majestic roar?

Or walked along a garden
and breathed the fragrant air
of multi colored flowers,
that bloom in splendor there?

The beauty of a rainbow
as it arc's across the sky.
almost takes my breath away.
Who could wonder why?

Have you sat with one you love
and watched the falling sun,
spraying rays of reddish haze
to show the day is done.

All the beauty that surrounds us
in this world whereon we trod,
is not from "Mother" nature,
but from our "Father"...**God**.

My Battle

I'm in the battle of my life.
The fight is from within;
But God is now my coach
and if I stay strong, I'll win.

My opponent is addiction
to drugs and alcohol,
and if lack real courage
he will win, and I'll lose all.

His manager is Satan,
the cunning, evil one.
But God's now in my corner
and the devil's on the run.

I have him up against the ropes
and feel God's strength within.
My family's on the front row cheering,
"Knock him out...and WIN!

Not Ready

*My spirit left my body
and I looked down to see
you and others weeping
while standing over me.*

*I cried out, "Here I am,
way up above your head!"
But you couldn't hear me
and I wondered… Am I dead?*

*I noticed that an angel
was near me standing by;
and said, "This can't be real,
I'm not ready yet to die."*

*She replied, 'I'm not surprised.
I hear that all the time,
from others who, just like you,
are still yet in their prime.'*

*I pleaded, "But I'm different.
I have lots of things to do.
Put me back into my body and
don't take me 'til I'm through.*

*I'll go to church each Sunday
and do the things I should.
If I must go today, my time
on earth won't look so good.*

(...Cont)

I'll say my prayers each evening
and spend time with family.
I'll give a little to the poor
and make God proud of me.

I'll be honest, kind, and caring
if He'll only let me stay.
I promise, I had planned
to make these changes anyway."

The angel said, 'I'm sorry.
This would all be great;
But after one has passed away,
it then becomes too late.'

Never have I felt such pain
and sorrow in my heart.
I began to tremble
and awakened with a start.

I realized I'd been dreaming
and felt joy beyond compare.
I leaped up from my bed
and fell upon my knees in prayer.

Either God, or my conscience,
helped me face reality.
And from that moment on
I knew there'd be a different me.

Oh Death, Where Is Thy Sting?

Oh death,
where is
thy sting?
Oh grave,
thy victory?

Praise Christ;
Savior Lord
and King,
who gave His
life for me.

(1 Corinthians 15: 55-57)

Oh My Savior

Oh my Savior, hear my plea.
Help me be all I can be.
Give me strength and courage too,
to live as Thou would have me do.

I thank Thee for Thy sacrifice.
How great the cost to pay the price.
A love that caused Thee to endure
such pain to bleed from every pour.

Thou died for me upon a cross.
Such depth of love puts me at loss.
I know that I cannot repay,
what Thou did for me that day.

But as I live and 'til I die,
with all my heart and soul I'll try.
and when it's time for us to meet;
Grateful tears shall wash Thy feet.

One's Worth

When my life has ended,
and my eulogy is read,
will I be deserving
if kind words of me are said?

Will tears of sadness fill the eyes
of those who knew me well,
as they contemplate my life
and bid me there farewell?

May God give me the wisdom,
in my life to always see;
It's how I live and how I love
that tells the worth of me.

I'm only one of many
In the world in which we live.
But I can make a difference
by the way I love and give.

When I see another,
who needs a helping hand;
I'll be there to show I care
in every way I can

Like the story of the starfish,
thrown back into the sea,
a difference can be made
by just one act of decency.

At every opportunity
I will plant a healing seed,
with a kind word, a smile,
and a hug for one in need.

Yes, I'm only one of many,
but with some help from you,
we'll make twice the difference..

...Care to make it two?

Our Daughter

As we contemplate the blessings
which are ours upon the earth;
We realize how great the one
who came to us through birth.

A daughter is a precious gift
from heaven up above.
She gives her parents meaning.
and fills their hearts with love.

Our dear, sweet loving daughter,
what a joy you truly are.
We will love you for forever,
whether near, or whether far.

We thank our Heavenly Father
who in his wisdom knew,
how wonderful our lives would be
when he blessed us with you.

Our Savior's Love

How much
do you love the Savior?
He died for you, you know.

He paid
a terrible price for you
because He loves you so.

He suffered
In Gethsemane,
and on a wooden cross,

He Died
an agonizing death
to save your soul from loss.

How can you repay Him?
There only is one way.
Live by all that He has taught,
And walk with Him each day.

Prayer For My Dad

Dear Lord, how can I thank You
for such special dad?
You must really love me,
'cause you gave the best you had.

You're my Father up in Heaven.
He's my father here on earth.
A greater dad, has no one had.
I've loved him since my birth.

May he receive the blessings
he is so deserving of.
And Lord, bless me to worthy be
of my dear Fathers' love.

Prayer For My Friend

I thank You Lord for giving me
a wonderful true friend.
You knew how much I'd need one,
and You knew just who to send.

A true friend who is always there
with willing helping hands.
A shoulder I can lean upon.
A heart that understands.

Lord, I pray You'll bless my friend
who gives so willingly.
And bless me too dear Lord, I pray,
an equal friend to be.

Prayer For My Mom

Dear Father up in Heaven,
bless my Mother here on earth.
You gave my spirit earthly life.
My mother gave me birth.

A special, loving angel,
sent down from up above.
She's a blessing to our family,
and fills our home with love.

Watch over her and keep her
in Thy tender loving care.
And thank You Lord for giving me
the best mom anywhere!

Precious Children

Dear Father up in heaven,
how ungrateful I would be,
If I failed to thank You
for the children given me.

I'll do my best to teach them
and to raise them in a way,
that they will live life worthy
to return to You one day.

Bless them in their journey
to be strong and never waiver,
but walk proudly in the footprints
of Christ, our loving Savior.

There are no greater blessings
that come from Thee above,
than those of precious children
to fill our lives with love.

"Q" and "A"

"Q"

Do our lives have purpose?
Is there a God above?
Will we live beyond the grave,
with those we dearly love?
Is there a place called heaven
where the good and righteous go?
Did Jesus Christ die on a cross,
because He loves so?

"A"

Through study, faith and prayer,
there is no need to guess.
All who SEEK God and His Son
will FIND the answer's... YES!

(Jeremiah 29: 13)
"And ye shall seek Me and find Me when
ye shall search for me with all your heart".

Raging Storms

In life there will be storms.
Small, and big ones too.
How we choose to weather them
is up to me and you.

We can let them rage inside us
to bring pain and misery ,
Or face with courage and with God,
all life's adversity.

We'll find that we grow stronger
and wiser with each trial.
So as they come into our life,
let's face them with a smile.

Satan's Lures

Satan loves the sport of fishing.
His tackle box filled with bait,
he goes out to the lake of life
to cast his line, and wait.

The devil knows us, every one,
and knows which lures to use.
In accordance with our weaknesses
he determines which to choose.

Dishonesty, pornography,
pride, selfishness and hate.
False witness, greed, the list goes on.
The sin becomes the bait.

Many bite and are deceived
and in a snap they're hooked.
They learn too late that Satan's bait
is not as it had looked.

God's given us the wisdom
and strength to do what's right.
When Satan tempts us with his lures,
show courage and don't bite.

Feed on Heavenly Father's words
and blessings will be yours,
as you pray, and stay away
from Satan ...and his lures.

Seize The Moment

It's Saturday morning. The grass needs mowed.
The garden needs weeding. The sink overflowed.
The garage is a clutter. The car needs repair.
He knows they need doing, but he doesn't care.

The roof has a leak and new shingles are waiting.
His list of "to-do's" are accumulating.
What's so important to warrant delay?
Does he think if ignored, they will just go away?

How can this man with so much on his plate
find good cause and reason to procrastinate?
It's because he's a man who is certainly wise.
A giant of a man in his Father, God's eyes.

A man who knows well his priorities,
and chooses the moments important to seize.
So where is this man with so much to be done?
He's in the backyard playing catch with his son.

Storms Of Sorrow

Today there will be rainclouds
with intermittent tears.
Some periods of sadness
until scattered heartache clears.

Dark clouds will hang over us
perhaps into the night.
But there are signs of clearing
and sunshine is in sight.

For God can change the weather
from heaven high above,
and turn our storms of sorrow
into sun-rays of His love.

Sun and Son

Our planet's source of energy
shines brightly from the sky.
Were it not for rays of sun
all life on Earth would die.

There is yet another "Son",
that shines from up above.
His light is even brighter
and fills the world with love.

The second rules the first
and is the greater of the two.
He is Christ, the Son of God.
Let His light shine for you.

Take My Hand

Dear Lord, in humbleness I pray
for guidance in my life each day.
That I may ever faithful be,
please take my hand and walk with me.

Should, in my weakness, I lose sight
of Thy great love and guiding light;
Stay beside me, Lord I pray,
and strengthen me along the way.

Then when I breathe my final breath
and close my eyes in earthly death;
May I not leave this world alone.
Lord, take my hand and walk me home.

Thanksgiving Table

The table is set for our thanksgiving feast
and all have taken their place
The meal of the year, is finally here,
and oh, how great it will taste..

Potatoes and gravy and cranberry sauce,
and rolls that are made fresh and hot.
Turkey with stuffing, right out of the oven.
Pumpkin pie that hasn't been bought.

Our family is anxiously gathered around
in a circle of love hand in hand.
A scene reminiscent of thanksgivings past.
A tradition we all understand.

Dad offers a prayer of thanksgiving to God
for abundance of blessings we share.
Tears touch his cheeks as he humbly gives thanks
for much more than the food that is there.

Though stomachs are empty, each heart is full
while united as family we pray,
Thanking dear God for His wonderful love,
and our blessings this Thanksgiving Day.

When this day is gone and life carries on,
may gratitude live on in me.
Lord help me, I pray, make every day
a day of thanksgiving to Thee.

The Awaited Visit

I went to a local rest home
to visit a friend I know;
And stopped to talk with a lady
who smiled and said hello.

She was happy I came over.
There was something she wanted to say.
She smiled her biggest smile, and said,
"My boy will come visit today.

He doesn't come too often,
but I'm sure he really tries."
And as she spoke, I could see
the pain deep in her eyes.

My heart was breaking for her
as she went on to say...
" In my prayers last night I ask...
That my boy would come visit today.

I'm lonely here in the rest home.
How I long for my son to stop by.
They say my health is failing,
but he'll visit before I die."

I leaned over and gave her a hug
and brushed her tears away.
She smiled and said, I'll be just fine.
My boy will come visit today

****

I wrote this poem after personally experiencing this conversation with a lonely lady at a rest home. A few weeks later, after another visit with my friend, I went to visit her again and learned she had passed away. I don't know if her son came for the awaited visit, but my heart was opened to the loneliness experienced by many of our elderly who spend the last chapter of their lives in rest homes and assisted care facilities.

The Cross

The cross is as an emblem
of my love, pure and true
and serves as a reminder
of my suffering for you.

For it was on a wooden cross I was nailed and lifted up.
And because of my great love for you, I drank the bitter cup.
The mind cannot perceive and there are no words to tell,
the greatness of My pain, as that hammer struck each nail.
I hung and died there on that cross, to ransom you from sin,
that when your life is over, heavens gate may bid you in.

Let not what I have suffered
be forgotten, or for naught,
but remember why I came
and remember all I taught.

Live each day in such a way
that all who know you see,
a kind and grateful Christian
who loves, and lives, for Me.

You are precious in my sight.
I saved your soul from loss.
So think how great My love
every time you see a cross.

The Dash Between

I knelt there at the headstone
of one I love and cried.
Name with dates of birth and death
were perfectly inscribed.

I pondered these two dates
and how little they both mean
when compared to the tiny dash
that lies there in between.

The dash serves as an emblem
of our time here on the earth
and although small, it stands for all
our years of life and worth.

And our worth will be determined
by how we live each day.
We can fill our dash with goodness,
or waste our life away.

(...Cont)

To ourselves, as well as others,
let's be honest, kind and true,
and live our lives in the way
we know God wants us to.

Let's look for opportunities
to do a worthy deed,
showing love and understanding
to those who are in need.

For If our hearts are full of love
throughout our journey here,
we'll, be loved by all who knew us
and our memory they'll hold dear.

And when we die, those memories
will bring grateful loving tears
to all whose lives were touched
by The Dash Between our years.

The Deceived

Be logical... there is no God,
or Jesus Christ, His Son.
And there is no afterlife
when life on earth is done.

There wasn't an atonement.
It's one big fairy tale.
There is no place called heaven,
and what's more, there is no hell.

Religion is just based on hope.
False hope that's one big lie.
So "Eat, drink, and be merry,
for tomorrow we shall die".

If all mankind were smart
and had wisdom, as I do;
All on earth would surely know
what is, and isn't true.

There is no God, or heaven.
We were all evolved instead
Life is for the living,
And when you're dead...you're dead.

* *

I'm sad for the vast many who believe the words above.
They haven't known the Father or His Son, and Their great love.

Man's wisdom can be ignorance and lead to one's downfall,
if they push aside their God who's the wisest of us all.

Corinthians, verse three eighteen speaks truth without disguise:
"Let no man deceive himself" in thinking he is wise.

The Departed Ship

It sailed into the sunset
on a glass-like sea of blue.
It's distance growing further
'til it disappeared from view.

One who stood beside me
softly whispered, "She is gone".
but in my heart, though unseen,
I knew the ship sailed on.

For, a ship on the horizon
disappearing in the night,
Is not one gone forever,
but only gone from sight.

Death is as a ship that sails
beyond where we can see,
to a place that God, our Father,
has prepared for you and me.

A place of peace and beauty
where loved ones gone before,
will rush in joy to greet us
on the day we reach it's shore.

Where heard by those awaiting
as our ship approaches near;
Not the whisper, "She is gone,"
but the joyful shout, "She's here!"

The Eraser

Do you know there's an eraser
that has hidden power within?
With just one swipe, it can wipe
away all of your sin.

The big ones and the small ones,
and the in-between ones too.
Just like magic, they'll be gone
and you'll be pure as new.

Its price was very costly
but do not be dismayed,
for it's offered free of charge
by one who greatly paid.

He's your Savior and Redeemer
and if you'll but repent,
He'll erase all of your sin
and it won't cost you a cent.

Heartfelt true repentance
will open Heaven's door,
and with it comes God's promise.
"I'll remember them no more."

(Jeremiah 31:34)

The Gardner

Story Of A Current Bush
(Inspired by the words of Hugh B. Brown)

*The gardener walked among the rows
beyond his garden wall,
and noticed a large current bush
standing proud, and tall.*

*With shears in hand he went to work,
this gardener, oh so wise,
and pruned the current bush down to
about one tenth it's size.*

*A bush that once was mighty,
now cut down stem by stem
and the gardener carefully listened
as the bush cried out to him..*

*"Just look, what you have done to me.
I used to stand so tall.
You've cut me down into a stump,
I'm nothing now at all.*

(Cont...)

(...Cont)

To others in the garden
what laughter I shall bring.
I thought you were the gardener.
How could you do this thing?"

'I am the gardener little bush,
and though you don't yet see,
I cut you down so you'll become
all you were meant to be'.

'I know it's hard, The gardener said,
but I did it for your good.
You've stopped producing fruit,
and are nothing more than wood.

You now have the potential
to become all you can be.
Rise up now, and bear great fruit
for all the garden to see.

The days rolled into weeks and months,
and how that bush did grow.
Beautiful blossoms turned to fruit,
covering it, high and low.

And as the gardener walked the rows
It came as no surprise
to see the current bush he'd pruned
now several times the size.

(Cont...)

"You've made me happy current bush.
I could not ask for more.
Yours is the best and sweetest fruit
that you have ever bore."

A very grateful current bush,
remembering grief expressed,
Cried, 'Master, please forgive me
for I truly have been blessed.

You stripped me of my useless pride
so I can clearly see ;
The wisdom of your pruning
has made a better me.

In the garden of our lives,
we have a Gardener too.
He's God, our Heavenly Father,
and He cares for me and you.

During times of great despair,
when everything seems wrong,
be patient and have faith,
for it is trials that make us strong.

Our Master knows what's best for us,
though we don't always see;
Sometimes in life we need cut down
to be all we can be!

The Godhead

The Father gave my spirit birth
as well as life upon the earth.

The Son died on a cross for me
that I might live eternally.

The Holy Ghost serves as my guide
and whispers to my soul inside.

They, to whom I owe the most;
are, Father, Son, and Holy Ghost.

The Grateful Leper

The Bible tells the story
of ten lepers, I recall.
They came with hope in Jesus
and He healed them, one and all.

But only one of all the ten
gave thanks on bended knee,
at the feet of Christ, who healed him
from his awful leprosy.

Do we show a grateful heart
to Father up above,
for the blessings that He gives us,
and His never-ending love?

Like the grateful leper
who returned on bended knee,
let's give thanks to Christ,
who gave His all for you and me..

The Greatest Gift Of All

When Christmas shopping is done,
wrapped gifts lie 'neath a tree
sparkling bright with tinsel and light
for everyone to see.

Each gift has been selected
with thoughtfulness and care.
Toys and such will mean so much
like all the gifts we bear.

But let us keep within our heart
the greater gift than these.
As gift of love, from up above,
should bring us to our knees.

A gift of birth to all on Earth.
A gift that's far from small.
To everyone, He gave His Son...
The greatest gift of all.

The Light Of Love

There's a light in the world
that's forever shining bright.
It can help us find our way
even in the darkest night.

It's power source is love,
and will never dim or wavier.
for it's the light of Jesus Christ.
Our precious Lord and Savior.

The Power Of Prayer

At the end of a day, I kneel and I pray,
to give thanks to my Father above.
How ungrateful I'd be if He didn't see
my gratitude for His great love.

Then when I arise, I look up to the skies,
and give thanks for the new day ahead.
For earth where I roam; Family and home
and the blessing of our daily bread.

My soul wants to shout, for I know beyond doubt
when I need Him, He'll always be there.
He's my God, my Friend, and with every "Amen",
I feel the great power of prayer.

Think Of These
For A-B-C's

A is for Atonement,
   and the Awful pain Christ bore.

B is for our Savior's Blood,
   that bled from every pore.

C for Christ, the Lord,
   and all he's done for you and me.

Think of this each time you hear
the letters... "A-B-C".

Thirty Pieces Of Silver

Store up Heaven's treasures
while here on earth below.
For wherein lies our treasure,
there will be our hearts also.

Let us not be blinded
by the world and led astray,
like Judas, the disciple,
who for silver did betray.

By choosing silver over Christ,
poor Judas, foolishly,
betrayed his Lord, with a kiss,
and sealed his destiny.

Many, as did Judas,
learn that greed comes with a price.
How foolish to love money
and riches more than Christ.

Such greed will but destroy
the soul and cause lament;
As did the thirty silver pieces
Judas never spent.

Tie A Knot and Hang On

Life can bring great challenges,
heartache and despair.
But keep the faith and know
that in our trials, God is there.

The sun shines after every storm
so never give up hope.
Tie a knot and hang on tight.
You're not yet out of rope.

The rope is as our earth life.
The only one we've got.
Our Savior's great atoning love,
is as the saving knot.

If we'll not give up hope,
thinking we're at our ropes end,
He'll be the knot that stops our fall,
and helps our lives to mend.

True To Who We Are

We're sons and daughters of God,
who loves His children so.
He's placed us here upon the earth
to help us learn and grow.

Let's be true to who we are
and act accordingly.
We're "Children of a living God".
Let's live worthily.

Walk The Walk

We can go to church each week.
Pray morning, noon, and night;
But it's not worth a sack of beans
If we're not living right.

Heavenly Father is not fooled
by those who Talk the talk,
but live their lives unwilling
to really Walk the walk.

"The walk" is showing kindness
and compassion every day
to those we find in need,
as we walk along life's way..

(Cont...)

(...Cont)

"The walk" is in the footsteps
of Christ... For it was He
who taught by His example
and then said, "Come follow Me."

"The walk" is in obedience
to our Father up above.
By keeping His commandments,
we are showing him our love.

"The walk" is straight and narrow
and takes us not to sin,
but leads us to life eternal
where we will live with Him.

May we always walk with God,
and with His loving Son.
And let it be that They will see;
Our talk and walk, are one.

Walk With Me

My heart is grieving on this day.
One I love has passed away.
Dear Lord, how grateful I would be
if for a time, You'll walk with me.

Just to know that You are near
will comfort every falling tear
and bring the peace I need and seek.
Without Thee I am just too weak.

Though with pain, I hurt and grieve,
in Thee, dear Lord, I do believe.
I know through You, this pain will flee.
Please take my hand and walk with me.

Walking With Our Savior

To learn the strength within us,
we were placed upon the earth.
Our book of life, when we return,
will show just what we're worth.
God knew in life we may get lost,
and so He sent His son.

Follow in His footsteps,
and walk with Him as one.

Our Savior's life should be our guide
to help along our way.
Stay close to Him through scriptures,
and read them every day.
Pray as soon as you arise,
and then when day is done.

(Cont...)

Follow in His footsteps,
and walk with Him as one.

Satan hopes to fool you,
with the many lies he'll tell.
He'll tempt, and try persuading you
by saying all is well.
So when he's on your shoulder,
knock him off and run.

Follow in Christ's footsteps,
and walk with Him as one.

He will never leave you,
if you'll just stay close to Him.
He'll walk with you and remain true
when life seems dark & grim.
And when this life is over
and you've walked with Him as one,

He will take you in his loving arms,
*and joyfully say, **"Well Done!"***

We Will Serve the Lord

Greater love hath no man,
than Christ, our Lord and King.
His life, and all He taught,
should mean more than anything.

Yet, for many in this world,
His teachings go ignored.
But As for me, and my house,
we will love and serve the Lord.

(Joshua 24: 15)

Wherein Lies Your Treasure?

Of all the treasures in our world,
It is known among the wise,
there is but one among them all
wherein true treasure lies.

Matthew 6: 21   It's not a large and fancy house
with luxury furnishings.
It isn't brand new golf clubs,
or a TV's massive screen.

It's not our job, or bank account,
fine jewelry, clothes or car.
These are only "things".
Let's not forget that's all they are.

For, if "things" become our treasure
selfness and pride will grow,
and "wherein lies our treasure,
there will be our heart also."

All the riches of the earth,
no matter large or small,
belong to God, our Father
but He loves "us" most of all.

May He bless us all
to be wise enough to see;
Our greatest earthly treasure
is a loving FAMILY!

Will You Live For Me?

Many martyrs have emerged
throughout each century.
Men and women, brave and bold,
have given all for Me.

If your life were on the line
would you defend what's true,
or deny... as did Peter,
I am one you knew?

I hung upon a cross,
and died in agony.
I ask but one thing in return.
Will you "live" for Me?

Wonderers & Seekers

Many wonder constantly
of life, and about death.
They wonder and they wonder
until their final breath.

While others seek for answers
with all their heart and mind;
Until they learn the many truths
that wonderers never find.

There's a five-letter word
these clues can help you find:
The answer isn't "known"
but to some, the word is "blind".

It's more valuable than gold,
yet free to everyone.
More powerful than a train,
with its engine on full run.

Although it isn't hidden
it is usually kept inside.
It is better than a compass
when you use it as a guide.

You either have it, or you don't.
There is no in-between
It puts meaning into life.
It is felt, but can't be seen.

It can mend a broken heart.
Cure disease. Even cancer.
It doesn't cost a dime,
and neither does the answer:

(Which is found on the next page:)

Faith

Woulda' Coulda' Shoulda'

I **Woulda'** followed the Savior
but was too wrapped up in me.
I **Coulda'** chosen right from wrong
but was too blind to see.

I **Shoulda'** been much stronger,
and spiritually more brave,
but, **Woulda', Coulda', Shoulda'**
went with me to my grave.

How I wish that these three words,
"Willing, Can, and Did"
were words that I had carried
all throughout my life instead.

You Are Loved

When you are sad and lonely
don't forget what you should know.
God, our Heavenly Father,
is nearby and loves you so.

He's placed us here, upon the earth,
and though He's up above,
He's promised He'll watch over us
and bless us with His love.

He knows, at times, life is hard.
Our Savior knows it too.
For it was here He suffered all
for love of me, and you.

Know that His great love for you
Is personal, and real.
There is no sorrow, hurt, or pain
our Father cannot heal.

Trust Him and reach out to Him.
through earnest heartfelt prayers.
You'll feel the comfort of His love,
and know how much He cares.

Your Journey

And now our walk of rhyme
has reached the pathway's end.
I hope you have enjoyed each step
as much as I, my friend.

May every pathway that you walk
throughout your journey here,
bring joy and happiness to you,
and those who you hold dear.

And may our Father, and His Son,
walk with you every day;
To guide you and bring joy,
Every footstep of the way.

– Ron Tranmer